EXPLOSIVE SCIENCE EXPERIMENTS FOR LITTLE CHEMISTS

SCIENCE PROJECT
CHILDREN'S SCIENCE EXPERIMENT BOOKS

BABY PROFESSOR
EDUCATION KIDS

Speedy Publishing LLC
40 E. Main St. #1156
Newark, DE 19711
www.speedypublishing.com

In this book, we're going to talk about some fun science experiments that explode. So, let's get right to it!

There are lots of experiments you can do at home or at school with some everyday ingredients. It's surprising that such ordinary things could make such big explosions but that's the power of chemical reactions! You should always have one or two adults supervising you when you perform experiments. When safety goggles are specified, everyone should be wearing them during exploding experiments! Some exploding experiments can be dangerous. Make sure that safety is always your top priority.

FRESH ORGANIC CRANBERRY JUICE

EXPERIMENT 1

EXPLODING CRANBERRY VOLCANO

Things You'll Need

- Three cups of pure cranberry juice—make sure that it's 100% cranberry juice otherwise the experiment won't work
- Baking soda

- Lemon juice from two lemons
- Five plastic cups that are clear
- A large glass baking pan with tall sides, so the mess won't go everywhere
- A tablespoon measuring spoon

SQUEEZING LEMON JUICE INTO SPOON

MEASURING CUP

- A measuring cup, the one cup size
- A flat table or workspace that won't be damaged by spilling cranberry juice
- A label for cup A, cup B, cup C, and cup D

STEPS TO TAKE

STEP ONE: Measure one cup of the cranberry juice and pour it into cup A. Repeat the process for cup B and cup C.

STEP TWO: Measure one cup of tap water and pour it into cup D.

STEP THREE: Ask an adult to help you cut and juice the lemons. Reserve their juice in another cup.

STEP FOUR: Place the three cups with juice into the glass pan. These are the ones that may overflow and get messy.

STEP FIVE: Measure two tablespoons of lemon juice into cup A. Compare the liquid in cup A to the liquid in cup B. Cup A has the lemon juice mixed into it and cup B doesn't. What do you notice about the addition of the lemon juice?

STEP SIX: Measure baking soda in the amount of one tablespoon and pour it into cup C. What happens when the baking soda mixes with the cranberry juice?

BAKING SODA

FOAM BUBBLE

STEP SEVEN: Allow the chemical reaction in cup C to go on for a few minutes. When the foam stops, observe the liquid in cup C. What happened to the color of the liquid in cup C? How much liquid is left in cup C?

STEP EIGHT: Wash off your measuring spoon completely so there isn't any baking soda left on it. Now measure out and add two tablespoons of lemon juice to cup C. What happens when the lemon juice reacts with the remaining liquid?

STEP NINE: Wait for the reaction of the lemon juice and liquid in cup C to be over. What happened in cup C after you added the lemon juice?

STEP TEN: Use your measuring spoon to add baking soda, about two tablespoons, to the cup with water. What happens when you add the baking soda to the water in cup D.

BAKING SODA AND WATER

FRESH CRANBERRIES

WHAT HAPPENED?

Cranberries contain an amazing pigment. It's called anthocyanin, which can tell you by its change in color whether something is an acid or a base. The anthocyanin gets darker when you added in baking soda because it is a base. It gets lighter in color when you added lemon juice, because it's citric acid.

The baking soda mixed with the cranberry juice, which is also slightly acidic, created the release of exploding bubbles because it's a reaction of the base, baking soda, with the tart acid from the cranberry juice. However, this doesn't always happen when baking soda is mixed with a liquid. If it's just mixed with water, it makes the water cloudy, but doesn't foam up. That's because water is pH neutral. It doesn't have any acid in it.

WHAT HAPPENED?

Cranberries contain an amazing pigment. It's called anthocyanin, which can tell you by its change in color whether something is an acid or a base. The anthocyanin gets darker when you added in baking soda because it is a base. It gets lighter in color when you added lemon juice, because it's citric acid.

The baking soda mixed with the cranberry juice, which is also slightly acidic, created the release of exploding bubbles because it's a reaction of the base, baking soda, with the tart acid from the cranberry juice. However, this doesn't always happen when baking soda is mixed with a liquid. If it's just mixed with water, it makes the water cloudy, but doesn't foam up. That's because water is pH neutral. It doesn't have any acid in it.

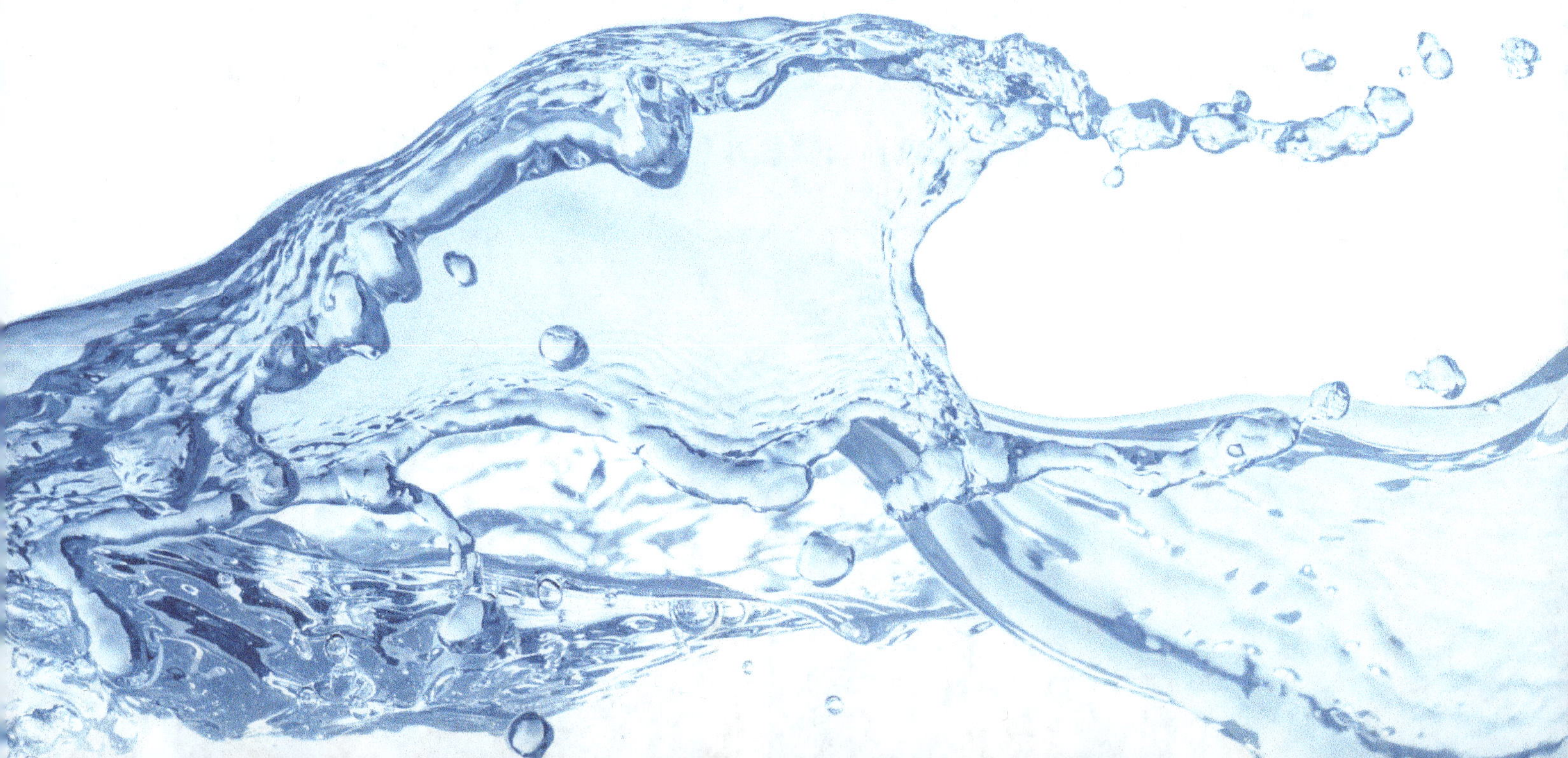

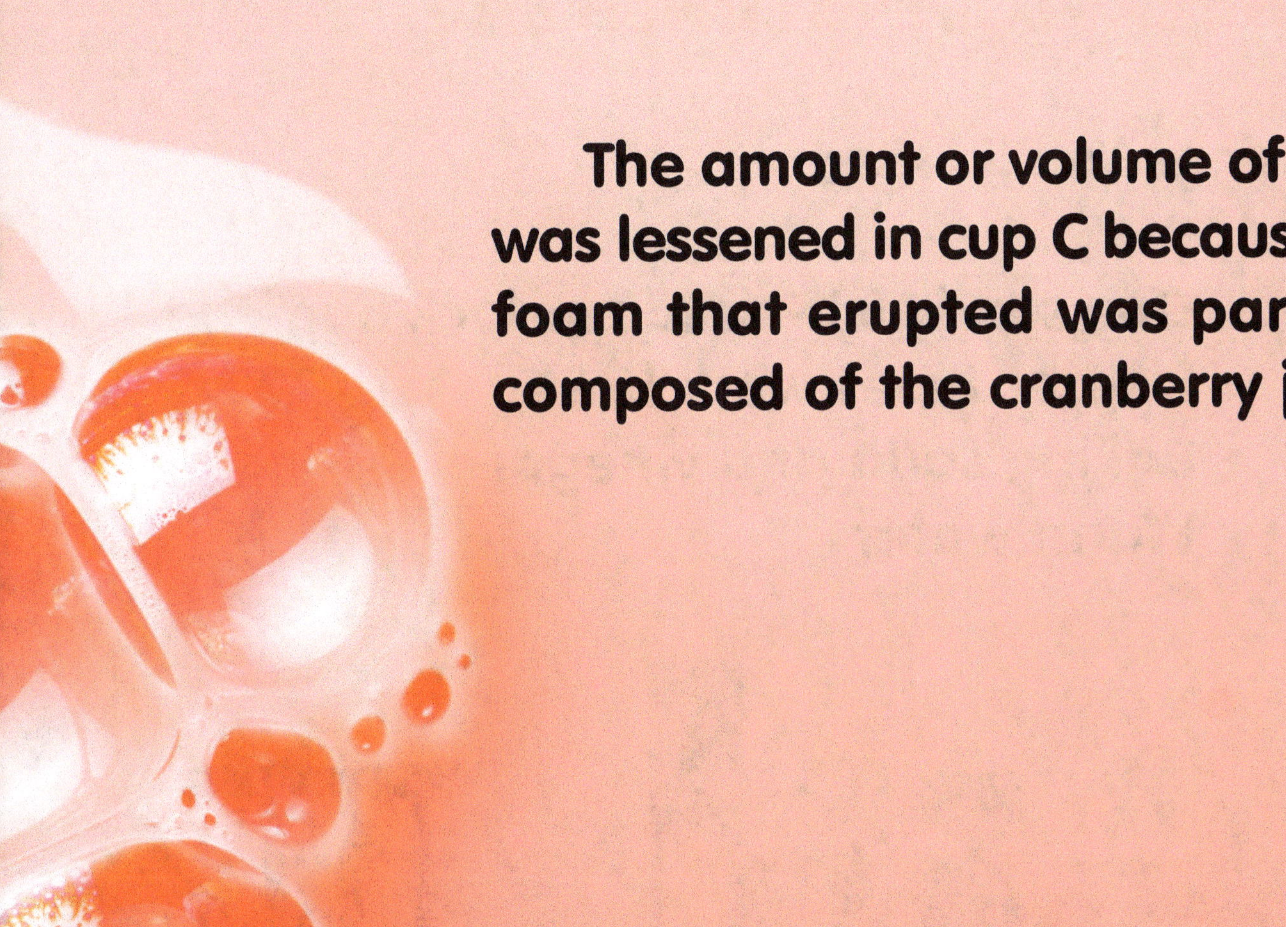

The amount or volume of juice was lessened in cup C because the foam that erupted was partially composed of the cranberry juice.

EXPERIMENT 2

THE EXPLODING LUNCH BAG

Things You'll Need

- One sandwich-sized zip-lock bag, the freezer types work best
- Baking soda and vinegar
- Warm water

vinegar
baking
soda

TISSUE

- A measuring cup
- A tissue
- Measuring spoons
- Safety goggles

STEPS TO TAKE

STEP ONE: Put all your materials near the kitchen sink or if your sink isn't large enough, do this outside. It's going to be messy!

STEP TWO: Measure one-quarter of a cup of warm water and pour it into the zip-lock bag. Make sure that your water is between very warm and hot.

KITCHEN SINK

ZIP LOCK

STEP THREE: Now, pour one-half of a cup of vinegar into the bag.

STEP FOUR: Put baking soda, about one tablespoon, into a piece of tissue and fold the tissue around it to make a packet.

STEP FIVE: Put on your safety goggles. Close the bag using its zip-lock, but leave just enough space to throw in the packet. Quickly throw the baking soda packet in and seal up the bag right away. Make sure that it's completely closed.

STEP SIX: Place the bag in the sink or outdoors on a flat surface. The bag will start blowing up from the chemical reaction and if it works the way it's supposed to, it will eventually explode! Stand back!

MAN WEARING SAFETY GOOGLES

CO2

WHAT HAPPENED?

By placing your baking soda in a packet, you've bought yourself some time before the baking soda and vinegar mix to create a chemical reaction. It's an acid-base reaction with the vinegar as the acid and the baking soda as the base. The two substances create the same gas we breathe out when we breathe, which is carbon dioxide.

Gases need lots of space to expand so the gas starts filling the bag and when it has nowhere else to go, the pressure causes the bag to burst. You can change the experiment by changing the temperature of the water and the amounts of vinegar and baking soda you use.

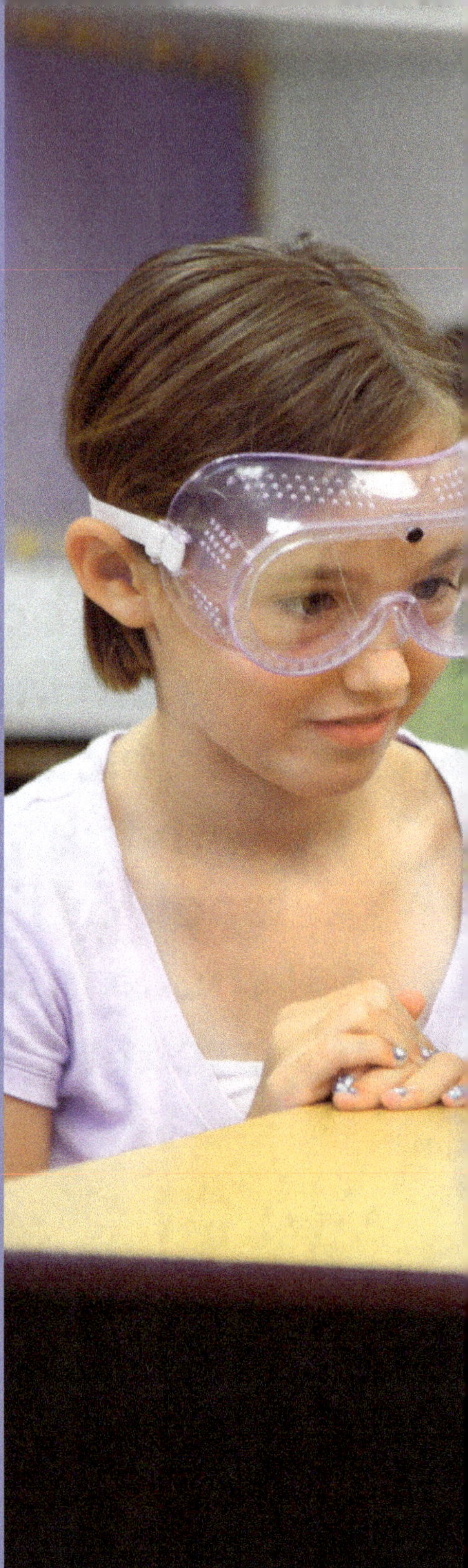

MILK

"FIREWORKS" WITH MILK

Things You'll Need

- Whole milk or buttermilk
- Food coloring

- **Clean cotton swabs—
Q-tips or another brand**
- **A shallow pan**
- **Dish soap**

PAN

STEPS TO TAKE

STEP ONE: Pour the milk or buttermilk into a shallow pan. Let the milk settle before you start the next step. Make sure that you have enough milk so that it has a depth of at least one-quarter of an inch.

STEP TWO: Add a drop or two of each of the colors of food coloring in the center of the milk. You should have red, yellow, blue, and green.

STEP THREE: Take a clean cotton swab and touch it to the center of the milk. Be careful not to stir or move the colors. Observe what happens.

FOOD COLORING

COTTON SWABS

STEP FOUR: Carefully drip some liquid dish soap onto a second cotton swab.

STEP FIVE: Now, place the swab with the liquid dish soap into the middle of the plate of milk and leave it there for at least 10 to 15 seconds. You should get exploding "fireworks" of different colors.

WHAT HAPPENED?

Even though milk or buttermilk contains a lot of water, it also has vitamins as well as proteins and minerals. In addition, it also includes tiny blobs of fat that are suspended in the liquid. Both proteins and fats are very sensitive to the liquid that surrounds them, which in this case is the milk.

The "fireworks" of color are caused by the droplet of liquid soap. Milk fat is described as a non-polar molecule, which simply means that even though it's suspended in the milk, it isn't dissolved. When the soap gets placed into the milk, the molecules in the soap start breaking up and collecting these non-polar molecules.

The polar surface of the soap structure joins with water molecules that are also polar and the fat is contained inside the soap structure. In other words, the fat, which is non-polar gets carried away by the water, which is polar. This is why dishwashing liquid is good at getting oil off your hands when water alone won't do the trick.

The fat molecules bend and twist in a "fireworks dance" as the molecules of soap race within the milk to connect with the fat molecules. While this is happening, the molecules of food coloring are shoved back and forth, left and right, which actually gives you a picture of the chemical reaction that's happening! The more fat the milk has, the more explosion of color you'll get.

SCIENCE EXPERIMENTS ARE FUN!

Science experiments are lots of fun, but you should make sure to have adults help you so you'll be safe. Use your science journal to record the results of your experiment. Write down what you think will happen before you perform the experiment. This prediction is your hypothesis. During and after the experiment, you can take notes on what you've observed. If you have a video camera, you can record the experiment while it's happening so you can observe it in more detail later. Once you perform an experiment successfully, you can alter some of the conditions to see if the results are different. By changing the experiment this way, you are using the scientific method to prove or disprove your hypothesis.

Awesome! Now that you've read about and performed some fun exploding science experiments you may want to read about some more awesome science experiments in the Baby Professor book From Floating Eggs to Coke Eruptions - Awesome Science Experiments for Kids | Children's Science Experiment Books.

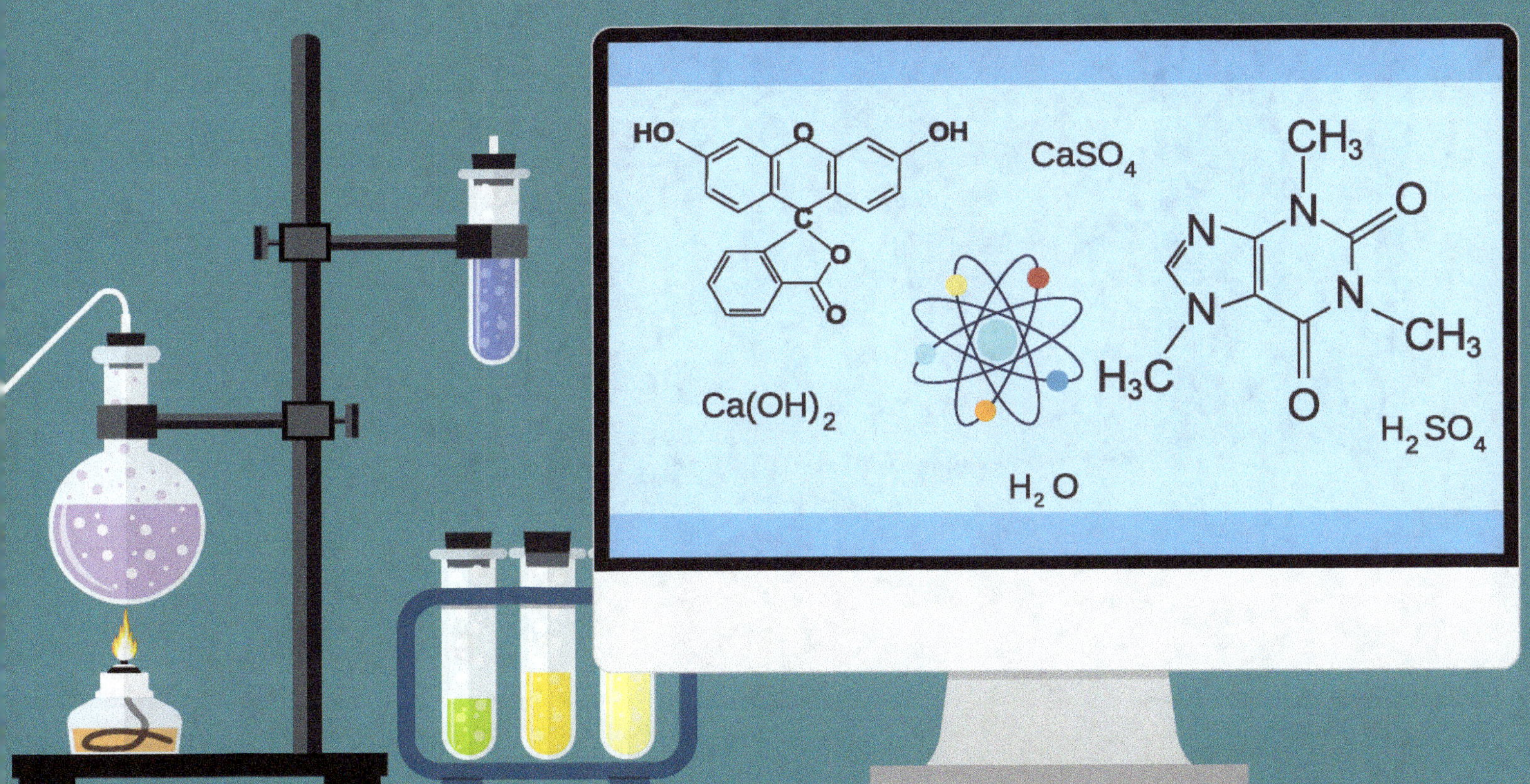
HO
OH
CaSO4
CH3
Ca(OH)2
H3C
CH3
H2SO4
H2O

www.ingramcontent.com/pod-product-compliance
Lightning Source LLC
LaVergne TN
LVHW060827170826
845678LV00010B/1919
* 9 7 9 8 8 6 9 4 3 5 5 8 3 *